What Does a Hammer Do?

by Robin Nelson

first step nonfiction

Lerner Publications Company · Minneapolis

What tool is this?

It is a hammer.

Tools help us do jobs.

Hammers make jobs easier.

This is the hammer's handle.

Hold on tight to the handle.

This is the **head** of a hammer.

The head pounds nails into wood.

The nails hold the wood together.

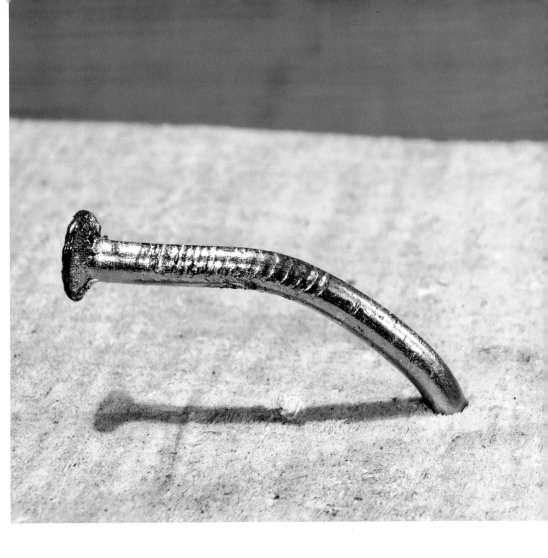

What if you want to take
out a nail?

This is the **claw** of the hammer.

The claw pulls nails out of wood.

A **carpenter** builds chairs
with a hammer.

Builders use hammers to make houses.

15

People use hammers to build tree houses.

What can you build with a hammer?

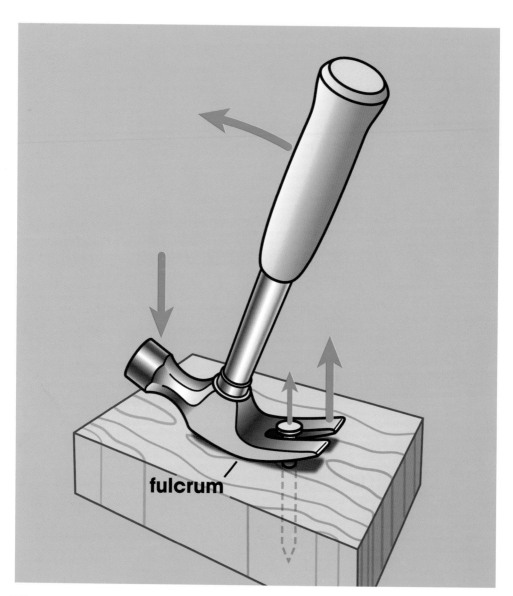

fulcrum

Hammers Are Levers

Hammers are simple machines. They are **levers**. A lever is a strong bar. People use levers to lift or pull something. The bar moves back and forth on a point called a **fulcrum**. You push or pull on one end of the bar, and the other end lifts a load.

See the nail sticking out of the wood? Hook the nail in the hammer's claw. Pull down on the handle. The hammer acts as a lever and pulls out the nail.

Safety First

 Ask a grown-up to help before using any tools.

 Wear safety glasses to protect your eyes.

 Roll up your sleeves. Tuck in your shirt. Tie back your hair. Take off any jewelry that might get in the way.

 Carry a hammer with the head down and away from your body.

Never run with a tool in your hand.

 Be careful not to pound your fingers. Use small taps to get the nail started.

 Put away the hammer and nails when you are done with your job.

Glossary

 carpenter – a person who builds things out of wood

 claw – the part of a hammer that pulls nails from wood

 fulcrum – the point where a lever moves

 head – the part of a hammer that hits something else

 levers – strong bars that are used to move things

Index

The images in this book are used with the permission of: © iStockphoto.com/Luis Pedrosa, p. 2; © Todd Strand/Independent Picture Service, pp. 3, 6, 7, 12, 22; © Stockbyte/Getty Images, p. 4; © wavebreakmedia ltd/Shutterstock.com, p. 5; © 5AM Images/Shutterstock.com, pp. 8, 22; © Anthony Berenyi/Shutterstock.com, p. 9; © Neale Cousland/Shutterstock.com, p. 10; © artiomp/Shutterstock.com, p. 11; © Steve Cukrov/Shutterstock.com, p. 13; © Mike Kemp/Rubberball/Getty Images, pp. 14, 22; © imagebroker.net/SuperStock, p. 15; © flashfilm/Taxi Japan/Getty Images, p. 16; © iStockphoto.com/Chris Fertnig, p. 17; © Laura Westlund/Independent Picture Service, pp. 18, 20, 21, 22.

Front cover: © sculpies/Shutterstock.com.

Main body text set in ITC Avant Garde Gothic Std Medium 21/25.
Typeface provided by Adobe Systems.

Lerner Publications Company
A division of Lerner Publishing Group, Inc.
241 First Avenue North
Minneapolis, MN 55401 U.S.A.

Website address: www.lernerbooks.com

Library of Congress Cataloging-in-Publication Data

Nelson, Robin, 1971–
        What does a hammer do? / by Robin Nelson.
            p.   cm. — (First step nonfiction—tools at work)
        Includes index.
        ISBN 978–0–7613–8976–7 (lib. bdg. : alk. paper)
        1. Hammers—Juvenile literature. I. Title.
    TJ1201.H3N45 2013
    621.9'73—dc23   2011039073

Manufactured in the United States of America
1 – BC – 7/15/12